BIOMES
of the World™

TUNDRA

Life in a Frozen Landscape

Greg Roza

rosen publishing's
rosen
central®

New York

For Autumn

Published in 2009 by The Rosen Publishing Group, Inc.
29 East 21st Street, New York, NY 10010

Library of Congress Cataloging-in-Publication Data

Roza, Greg.
Tundra: life in a frozen landscape / Greg Roza.—1st ed.
　　p. cm.—(Biomes of the world)
Includes bibliographical references.
ISBN-13: 978-1-4358-5002-6 (library binding)
ISBN-13: 978-1-4358-5428-4 (pbk)
ISBN-13: 978-1-4358-5434-5 (6 pack)
1. Tundra ecology—Juvenile literature. 2. Tundras—Juvenile literature.
I. Title.
QH541.5.T8R69 2009
577.5'86—dc22

2008022262

Manufactured in the United States of America

On the cover: The Siberian tundra. (*Inset*) Local flora in the Siberian tundra.

CONTENTS

INTRODUCTION

Biomes are Earth's major wildlife communities. The biomes of the world include coniferous forests, deciduous forests, deserts, grasslands, oceans, and tundra. Biome climates depend on several criteria, primarily latitude, or where they are situated on the north/south axis of Earth. Different areas in the same latitude around the world can feature vastly different biomes based on humidity, wind patterns, and elevation.

Biomes are often described by the major plant groups that can be found in them, such as coniferous trees in the taiga biome or cacti in the desert biome. A biome is also characterized by the adaptations that plants and animals have developed to allow them to survive there. For example, zebras of the grassland biome have black and white stripes, which act as camouflage. Lions, a main predator of zebras, are color-blind. Therefore, they have difficulty seeing zebras when they are standing in tall grass or behind tree branches.

The tundra is Earth's coldest and most fragile biome. It is also the biome with the fewest plant and animal species. Most of Earth's tundra is located around the North Pole in an area called the Arctic. Tundra can also be found near the tops of tall mountains and in the Antarctic.

Reindeer, like the one shown here, are common to Arctic tundra areas around the world.

Plants and animals living in the tundra have developed some of the most unique and interesting adaptations of Earth's species. However, due to recent changes caused by climate fluctuations as well as human activities, much of the tundra is at risk today.

In this book, we will learn what makes the tundra so unique. We will also learn about the dangers threatening the tundra and what we can do to help.

CHAPTER 1

WELCOME TO THE TUNDRA

The word "tundra" comes from a word used by the native people of the Scandinavian tundra. It means "treeless plain." Few trees grow in the tundra because of low temperatures and a short growing season. It is the coldest and driest biome on Earth. Some scientists even consider the tundra a type of desert because it usually receives less than 10 inches (25.4 centimeters) of precipitation a year in the form of snowfall.

Tundra biomes can be found on all of Earth's continents. Some people think of a snow-covered plain when they hear the word "tundra." Others may think of a cold mountaintop. That is because there are two kinds of tundra.

The tundra is the youngest of Earth's biomes. The most recent ice age ended about ten thousand years ago. During the ice age, much of the Northern Hemisphere was covered with glaciers. As Earth slowly warmed, the ice receded north. The tundra we are familiar with today had formed around seven thousand years ago.

The land of the tundra was the last to be uncovered by receding glaciers. The soil in warmer regions had many years during which to form. Plant roots, insects, burrowing animals, and microorganisms keep the soil churned up in warmer climates.

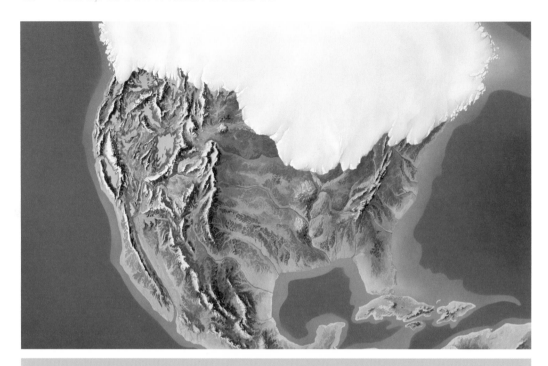

During the last ice age, glaciers covered a large portion of Earth's Northern Hemisphere and reached as far south as the Ohio River and even carved out the Great Lakes.

The soil of the tundra is frozen for most of the year, and these processes are not able to take place as often in warmer places.

The Arctic Tundra

The Arctic tundra, as its name suggests, is mainly around the North Pole and some areas around the South Pole. The tundra in the Southern Hemisphere is often referred to as the Antarctic tundra. Both kinds of tundra are called polar tundra.

The Arctic tundra covers about 20 percent of Earth's surface, including land in Russia, China, Canada, the United States (Alaska), Greenland, Iceland, Finland, Norway, and Sweden. The tundra is usually located between 55 and 70 degrees north latitudes. This far north, the sun does not rise for weeks at a time during winter because Earth is tilted away from it. The temperature can be as low as –75° Fahrenheit (–59° Celsius) in the winter. The sun stays in the sky for weeks during the summer months. The temperature usually climbs no higher than about 50° F (10° C) in the summer. Average yearly temperatures for the Arctic tundra are about –18° F (–28° C).

The boundary where the taiga biome and the tundra begin is called the tree line. Most trees and shrubs cannot survive beyond this boundary because the top layer of soil is frozen for

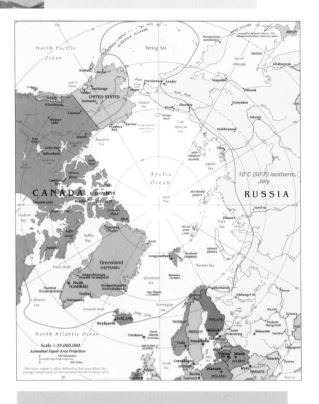

This map of Earth's northern pole shows where the Arctic tundra is located.

most of the year. The tundra soil remains permanently frozen from about 1 to 10 feet (.3 to 3 meters) below the surface. This layer, called permafrost, keeps water from draining away in the summer. The northernmost boundary of the tundra is the line past which no plants can grow.

The tundra winter lasts from September to April or May. During the short summer season, temperatures may get up to about 50° F (10° C). The top layer of permafrost usually thaws during this time, creating soggy marshes. Many insects hatch and breed during the summer, attracting many types of migrating birds.

THE ANTARCTIC TUNDRA

The Antarctic tundra is a much less extensive tundra-like region around the South Pole. Much of Antarctica is always covered with ice—sometimes as deep as 3.1 miles (5 kilometers). Most of it is a bleak land where very few or no organisms survive.

The Antarctic tundra appears mainly on islands and on parts of the Antarctic Peninsula. Antarctica's two vascular plants can be found there, as well as seals, penguins, seabirds, and plentiful fish. About 14 to 20 inches (35 to 50 cm) of precipitation falls on this area per year, mostly in the form of rain in the summer months. The temperatures do not fall as low as in the Arctic tundra. In fact, the northernmost islands are free from permanent ice.

The Alpine Tundra

The Alpine tundra exists on the tops of mountains and high plateaus around the world. It is named after the Alps, a mountain range in Europe. Alpine tundra occurs in Africa, Asia, Europe, North America, South America, and New Zealand. The Alpine tundra climate resembles that of the Arctic tundra because of its high altitude.

The boundary where the forest biome ends and the Alpine tundra begins is marked the tree line. Alpine tree lines are different depending on the location. Tree lines in the Alps vary between 5,000 and 9,000 feet (1,524 and 2,743 m). The Himalaya Mountain Range in Asia is the world's highest Alpine tundra, as well as the

Tombstone Territorial Park, located in the Yukon territory of Canada, has a wide range of wildlife. The northern section of the park is the southernmost boundary of the arctic tundra. The mountains of this area feature the alpine tundra.

southernmost Alpine tundra in the Northern Hemisphere. The tree line in the Himalayas starts at about 13,000 feet (3,962 m).

Alpine tundra is usually a dry biome, although snowfall can be heavy at times. Winter can be snowy, bleak, and very cold. In summer, the land can be rocky or covered with short grasses and lush wildflowers. The Alpine tundra rarely has permafrost, and the ground features good drainage. The highest Alpine tundra can be covered with snow all year round. There are usually fewer plants and animals in the higher Alpine tundra because the air is thinner, making it difficult for animals to get oxygen and plants to get carbon dioxide.

CHAPTER 2

THE NONLIVING ENVIRONMENT

Earth revolves around its axis—an imaginary line running straight through the planet's center from the North Pole to the South Pole. It is Earth's rotation that causes day and night. Our seasons occur because of the tilt of Earth's axis. During winter, the Northern Hemisphere is tilted away from the sun. The sun does not rise on the Arctic tundra for several months, making it the coldest and darkest biome on Earth.

During summer, the Northern Hemisphere is tilted toward the sun. The sun does not set on areas of the Arctic tundra for several months, and, for this reason, these areas are sometimes called the "Land of the Midnight Sun." Constant sunlight allows much of the surface ice to melt and form lakes for migrating wildlife. The summer warmth doesn't last very long, though. By late June, the North Pole begins to lean away from the sun again, and soon the ice returns.

Arctic Tundra Climate

In the winter, the tundra is a seemingly lifeless expanse of ice. The temperature can drop as low as –70° F (–57° C). Little precipitation falls in the tundra—some areas receive less than 5 inches (13 cm) a year. Very little moisture evaporates in the tundra during the winter. The bitter temperatures are enough to keep the tundra covered with ice for most of the year. Swift Arctic winds can make the temperature seem much lower than it really is.

The warmer weather brings water and life to the tundra. Migrating animals stop by pools of water that have formed from melting ice and snow. Plants, insects, and birds use the warmth and water to breed quickly before winter returns. On a rare summer day, temperatures may rise as high as 70° F (21° C).

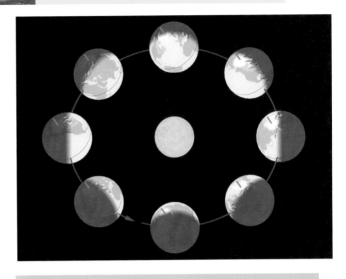

This image shows how much sunlight the Arctic tundra gets throughout the year due to its position relative to the sun.

Alpine Tundra Climate

Just as the temperature drops the closer you get to Earth's poles, it also drops the higher the elevation. For this reason, many tall mountains and plateaus feature tundra-like weather conditions. Alpine tundra around the world begins at different elevations.

As warm, moist air rises in elevation when it meets a mountain, the decreasing temperature causes the wind to release its moisture in the form of rain and snow. This can result in high snowfall in the windward, or wind-facing, Alpine tundra. Wind usually dumps most of its moisture before it passes over a mountain. This means that the other side of the mountain is often drier than the windward side.

Tundra Soil

Bacteria are needed to break down dead organic matter into the basic nutrients that plants need to grow. Since the tundra is frozen

TUNDRA CLIMATES AROUND THE WORLD

Place	Location	Average Yearly Precipitation	Average High Temperature	Average Low Temperature
Barrow, Alaska	320 miles (515 km) north of Arctic Circle	4.6 inches (11.6 cm)	40° F (4° C)	–23° F (–31° C)
Khatanga, Russia	500 miles (805 km) north of Arctic Circle	13 inches (33 cm)	55° F (13° C)	–34° F (–37° C)
St. Moritz, Switzerland	Swiss Alps, 6,089 feet (1,856 m) above sea level	20 inches (50.8 cm)	53° F (12° C)	16° F (–9° C)
Deception Island, Antarctica	About 75 miles (120 km) north of Antarctic Peninsula	22.2 inches (56.4 cm)	37° F (3° C)	11° F (–12° C)

most of the year, there is very little bacterial activity in the soil. Slow decomposition of vegetation results in the buildup of a matted layer of dead vegetation called humus. Nutrients remain locked in humus. This results in soil that is very low in nutrients, which makes it less capable of sustaining a variety of plants. Some areas are covered with peat, which is partially decomposed organic matter that is rich in carbon dioxide. Peat is good for plants, and people can use it for fuel.

Tundra soil covered with snow and ice for most of the year remains frozen. In some areas of northern Canada, the permafrost is more than 2,100 feet (640 m) thick. Scientists believe that it took about ten thousand years for the soil to freeze this deep. In summer, the upper layer of the soil becomes soft and spongy. This layer is called the active layer because all of the plant growth occurs there. In the coldest areas, the active layer is about 20 inches (50.8 cm) thick. In warmer areas, it can be 35 inches (88.9 cm) thick.

During the short summer season, the ice and snow of some areas of the Arctic tundra melt to form numerous small rivers and lakes.

In the summer, the active layer is difficult to walk on. Many areas are covered with pools of water and marshy land that attracts many insects. Wet surface soil sometimes slides downhill over deeper permafrost, causing ripples on hillsides.

Polygons, Palsas, and Pingos

The cycle of freezing, thawing, and refreezing of soil and rocks causes unique geological features in the Arctic tundra. Much of the tundra features a craggy and rocky landscape. The fluctuating temperatures and extreme cold cause the ground to swell and crack. Cracks formed in the winter fill up with water, which in turn freezes the next winter. As this process continues, the cracks become wider

Tundra polygons, shown here in Nunavut, Canada, range in size from 5 or 6 feet (about 2 m) across to 150 feet (46 m) wide. They're separated by ice.

and the ground becomes uneven. This results in the appearance of geometric shapes in the ice and soil. Scientists usually call these shapes polygons.

Over several years, cracks grow wider and fill with more and more ice. The soil is squeezed upward on either side of an ice wedge, eventually forming loose piles of rock and soil. It can also cause peat-covered ice mounds called palsas. Most palsas grow to about 3 feet (.9 m) high. Occasionally, they grow as high as 32 feet (9.7 m). Palsas often grow in groups on wet tundra.

Palsas form when frozen water at the core draws in more water from the surrounding area, causing them to grow. Peat, soil, and minerals that cover palsas act as insulation during the summer, which keeps the ice core from melting. Once a palsa grows large enough, the outer covering breaks and falls away. Exposed to the sun, palsas melt and leave small basins in the ground.

The ice wedges that cause palsas also cause formations called pingos. Pingos form most often in areas where the tundra permafrost has thawed to create numerous shallow lakes. The ground beneath these lakes often remains unfrozen because the ice and water above them act as insulation against the cold air. When the shallow lakes dry up or drain away, they leave a basin. A new layer of permafrost forms on the lower ground. The soil beneath the permafrost remains unfrozen. The

In this photograph are two pingos in the Northwest Territories located in Canada.

unfrozen soil becomes enclosed on all sides by ice and permafrost. The resulting pressure forces water in the soil upward, where it quickly freezes. As more water is forced upward, a dome begins to form beneath the permafrost and humus.

The water from one thawed lake may feed into a nearby pingo. Nearby rivers and streams, thawing glaciers, and melting snowfall may also feed into pingos. This constant addition of water causes the pingo to grow larger. The average pingo is about 650 feet (198 m) in diameter, but it may grow to about 1,950 feet (594 m). The largest one is about 157 feet (48 m) tall. Eventually, pingos become too heavy or their source of water is disrupted, and they collapse. However, they may last for one thousand years before this actually happens.

CHAPTER 3

THE LIVING ENVIRONMENT

Biomes are often defined by the types of plants and animals that they support. The tundra is sometimes defined by its lack of wildlife. However, tundra wildlife is specially adapted for life in the coldest biome on Earth.

Arctic Tundra Plants

There are about 228 species of plants in the Arctic tundra. Permafrost prohibits plant roots from reaching very deep. Most plants don't grow taller than 8 inches (20.3 cm). Their small size helps them to conserve heat and moisture. Many plants get the carbon dioxide that they need for photosynthesis from the peat in which they grow. In the winter, plants are buried beneath the snow, which keeps them insulated against the harsh Arctic climate. About 99 percent of plants in the Arctic tundra are perennials. This is important because tundra plants don't always produce seeds every year.

The most common kinds of plants in the Arctic tundra are mosses, grasses, and sedges. These plants grow low to the ground in thick clumps and provide a stable foundation for other plants. Trees found in the tundra, such as dwarf willows and black spruces, are usually withered, bent, and solitary. Trees

Dryad flowers (*top*), Bearberry, and Dwarf Birch (*bottom*) are all hardy plants that can survive the harsh conditions of the Arctic tundra.

Here, lichen grows in the White Mountains National Recreation Area near Fairbanks, Alaska.

grow wider than they do tall, and their roots spread out within the active layer.

Arctic flowers begin to bloom as soon as the snow begins to melt. Colorful wildflowers—such as buttercups, red paintbrushes, and Arctic lupines—blanket large areas of the tundra with small, hardy blossoms. Berries brighten the banks of streams and lakes. The leaves and flowers of many Arctic tundra plants are dark green. This allows them to absorb the sun's heat and light more effectively. Many develop rough, leathery leaves that can hold more water.

Tundra Lichens

Lichen is a mixture of a fungus and an alga. The fungus collects water and nutrients from the ground, and the alga uses photosynthesis to make food. Lichens can look like stalks, leaves, shrubs, or moss.

There are approximately 2,500 tundra lichens. They are often the first organisms to develop on bare ground. They help seal water in the soil, making it a suitable foundation for other plants. They also help make the soil less likely to erode. Eventually, lichens break down the surfaces on which they grow. They can even break down rock. This helps create new soil. Many tundra animals depend on lichens for food.

Lichens grow incredibly slowly, usually less than one millimeter a year. When they are destroyed, it can have a devastating effect on

When approached by enemies, adult musk oxen form a circle around the young facing out. This is an effective defense against some predators, such as Arctic wolves, but it makes them easy prey for human hunters.

the rest of the tundra. Without lichens, life in the tundra would be much harder—perhaps impossible—for other plants and animals.

Mammals in the Tundra

Only about sixty species of mammals live in the tundra. Perhaps the most recognizable tundra mammal is the polar bear. This white bear has two layers of fur to keep it warm and dry. It has a thick layer of fat that keeps it warm and makes it more buoyant in water. The polar bear's muzzle is long, which enables it to catch prey—mostly seals—through holes in sea ice. Polar bears swim well; they travel by moving from ice floe to ice floe. In the summer, it is more difficult for

LEMMINGS

Much of the tundra ecosystem revolves around a species of rodent called the lemming. They eat grasses, sedges, roots, and lichens. In the summer, lemmings dig burrows in the soft active layer for roots to eat and to find shelter from their many predators. They continue to use these burrows in the winter.

Lemming populations generally rise and fall in three- or four-year cycles. At the peak of this cycle, there are often enough lemmings to clear an entire area of plant life. This is bad for other herbivores, but it's good for predators that eat lemmings, such as snowy owls. When lemmings run out of food to eat, they migrate in large groups to new areas. When the lemming population is at a low point, the number of herbivores surges. Animals that eat lemmings usually move away or experience a drastic drop in numbers.

Lemmings are closely related to mice, rats, gerbils, and hamsters.

polar bears to find food because there is less ice to stand on. Polar bears spend part of the short summer season hibernating, although they are able to wake up quickly to search for food.

Musk oxen roam plains in packs of ten to twenty searching for lichens and grasses. They have two layers of heavy fur to protect them against the subzero temperatures. Although musk oxen are the only herd mammals endemic to the tundra, others come and go based on migratory patterns and weather conditions. Depending on the region, caribou, reindeer, and moose can also be found roaming the tundra.

Other tundra mammals include the Arctic fox and the Arctic hare. Both have mostly brown fur in the summer. In the winter, both mammals shed their brown coats and grow white coats. This allows them to blend in with their surroundings during each season. Arctic hares can hide from predators, such as wolves and foxes. Arctic foxes are adept at stalking lemmings and birds.

The Boloria selene butterfly (*above*) thrives in the marshes of the North American tundra.

Tundra Insects

The tundra is home to an amazing variety of insects: bees, beetles, moths, flies, mosquitoes, and many others. Most tundra insects have small, dark bodies that enable them to absorb and use sunlight effectively. In the winter, many tundra insects hibernate. Some insects freeze solid and then resume life when they thaw in the summer. Others have a chemical that lowers the freezing point of water in their bodies, which allows them to withstand the subzero temperatures.

In the summer, insects lay their eggs near small lakes and marshes. When the eggs hatch, dense clouds of insects hover over the plains. Other insects lay eggs that freeze during the long winter, then thaw out and hatch in the spring. Many kinds of spiders, particularly the wolf spider, stalk insects on the ground.

The kea, shown here, is well known as an intelligent bird. Kea eat a wide variety of plants and animals. They have even been known to attack sick sheep.

Birds in the Tundra

The Arctic tundra is home to about 285 species of birds, including ptarmigans, snow geese, jaegers, snowy owls, and long-tailed ducks. Most birds visit the tundra in the summer to feed on the plentiful insects. The wetlands make a good breeding ground for Arctic birds.

Very few birds spend the entire winter in the tundra. The willow ptarmigan and the rock ptarmigan are the most common year-round tundra birds. Like the Arctic hare and Arctic fox, ptarmigans shed their feathers several times a year and grow a new coat that helps them blend in with their seasonal surroundings.

Wildlife in the Alpine Tundra

Wildlife in the Alpine tundra is often very similar to that in the Arctic tundra, but it can vary from region to region. Bogs and lakes that attract swarms of insects and birds are common. Alpine tundra plants include mosses, sedges, and lichens. Many large predator birds can be found in the Alpine tundra, such as the gyrfalcon—the largest falcon in the world. They feed on rodents and smaller birds. The Alpine tundra of New Zealand is home to the kea, the world's only Alpine parrot. Gelada baboons live in the tundra of Ethiopia. Depending on the region, other Alpine animals include bears, mountain goats, antelope, llamas, lynx, wolves, wolverines, and reindeer, to name a few of the most common species.

Wildlife in the Antarctic Tundra

Life in the Antarctic tundra is very different from that in the Arctic and Alpine tundra. There are only two main types of vegetation in the Antarctic: lichens and mosses, and grassland. The soil is poor and does not sustain many vascular plants. Some plants live in the cracks of rocks. There is more wildlife variety on the islands around Antarctica. South Georgia Island is home to the largest concentration of nesting animals in the world. In the summer, the coast is crowded with penguins, seals, and seabirds. These animals get their food from the ocean. The only ones that stay in the Antarctic tundra all year long are insects, including mites, spiders, springtails, nematodes, and moths. One species of Antarctic mite is the southernmost animal in the world. It feeds on organic particles blown south by the strong winds.

CHAPTER 4

THE HUMAN PRESENCE

People have been living in the Arctic tundra ever since the last ice age ended. Most native tundra peoples share similar languages, cultures, and modes of survival. Natives of the North American tundra migrated there from Asia via the Bering Strait. Life in the tundra has never been easy, but, like plants and animals, people have adapted to the harsh living conditions. Most people of the tundra were nomads traveling in search of food.

The Inuit are native to the tundra of Canada, Greenland, and the United States. The Sami live in the Scandinavian and Russian tundra. The Khants, Nenets, Komi, and Chuckchi live in the Siberian tundra of Russia. Although most of these groups utilize modern technology for hunting, building, and survival, they still rely heavily on ancient methods and traditions.

Changing the Tundra

Although the Inuit and other native people still practice the traditions and survival techniques of their ancestors, their lives today are often very different. Modern industry has caused great changes to the tundra. It has brought money and modern conveniences to their communities, making their lives easier.

Many Inuit still enjoy a traditional game called the blanket toss, as seen in this photograph. The "blanket" is traditionally made of seal and walrus skins. The person who is tossed the highest wins.

THE INUIT

The Inuit have lived in the North American tundra for about one thousand years. The word "Inuit" means "people" in their native language. The Inuit survived for centuries using ancient techniques. They hunted land animals and whales for food and clothes, and they made tools and weapons from bone, ivory, and stone. They made homes called igloos from ice. They also made tents from animal hides. Europeans first made contact with the Inuit in the 1500s as they searched for a northwest passage to Asia. They gave the Inuit iron, which they used to make improved fishing and hunting tools.

Today, there are about ninety thousand Inuit in the tundra, which makes them the largest Arctic ethnic group. Half live in Greenland, and half live in Alaska and northern Canada. In 1999, the Canadian government established the territory of Nunavut in northeast Canada. This area, which was formally part of the Northwest Territories, has been home to the Inuit people for centuries. "Nunavut" is Inuit for "our land."

Modern industry has also caused great damage to the tundra. The increasing human population has resulted in a decrease of animal species as they are hunted for food. Pollution from the construction and operation of factories, oil wells, refineries, and mines has resulted in the decline of plant and animal species. Other pollutants, such as pesticides, can get into the water supply and harm many animals.

Development of urban areas and roads in the tundra is relatively new. The first roads and buildings constructed in the tundra were often

Illulissat is a settlement on the west coast of Greenland. The nearby Illulissat glacier is the fastest moving in the world, expanding 66–98 feet (20–30 m) a day. The glacier doubled its speed between 1997 and 2003.

built directly on the permafrost. Once these structures were completed, many of them sank into the permafrost as it melted beneath them. This resulted in cracked roads and crumbling building foundations. Now, builders use refrigeration to keep the permafrost frozen beneath buildings. However, too much damage has already been done.

Hunting and Whaling

Arctic nomads used the animals they caught for food, shelter, clothing, tools, and fuel. Non-native people began coming to the tundra to fish and hunt shortly after Europeans began settling in North America. Sailors and fishermen came to Alaska and Greenland beginning in the 1600s to fish and hunt whales. Hunters killed about

Sport hunting brings in a lot of money for the Inuit people of Nunavut, Canada, but it also reduces the number of wild animals, such as this walrus, in the area.

one thousand whales a year in these areas until they were almost extinct. In the 1700s, European hunters drastically reduced the population of seals. Prior to the arrival of the Europeans, the Inuit had hunted seals for hundreds of years.

Musk oxen were hunted to extinction in Europe, Asia, Alaska, and most of Canada by the mid-1800s. The remaining musk oxen in Canada and Greenland were used to repopulate other areas. Today, there are about forty thousand musk oxen in Canada and about one thousand in Alaska. There are laws today against hunting musk oxen and other tundra animals. Caribou were almost wiped out, too, in North America. They are also slowly growing in number, thanks to these laws.

THE ARCTIC NATIONAL WILDLIFE REFUGE

The Arctic National Wildlife Refuge (ANWR) is a 19.2-million acre wilderness untouched by human development. This refuge contains glaciers, meadows, wild rivers, and boreal forests. It encompasses six ecological biomes, including the Arctic and Alpine tundra. It is home to the largest variety of wildlife around the Arctic Circle. The refuge is a vast and wild area with a single gravel road linking it to the rest of the world. The ANWR is a national treasure, as well as the homeland of several Native American peoples. The area became a federally protected refuge in 1960.

Prudhoe Bay, which is just east of the refuge, is currently North America's largest oil field. In recent years, the U.S. government has considered loosening the federal restrictions on the ANWR to allow oil drilling. Some Americans—including a large portion of the Native American population in the area—think it is a good way to make money and get cheaper fuel for the United States. Others protest oil drilling in the ANWR because of the negative effects that it will have on the tundra. Constructing roads, power plants, and buildings will destroy much of the pristine land and native species. The argument is still ongoing.

Oil Drilling

Most cars, trucks, planes, and ships require oil and gasoline to function. Oil and gas are also used in factories and plants and in the production of many products, including plastics. Oil comes from deep within Earth's crust. In order to reach this supply of oil, people need to build oil wells. Drilling for oil in the tundra began in

This is a British Petroleum (BP) oil field in Prudhoe Bay. BP began to close down this facility in August 2006 because of an oil leak that was caused by corroded pipelines.

Prudhoe Bay in the 1960s. This practice has had a devastating effect on the tundra.

Before oil drilling begins, people must build roads to bring in vehicles, equipment, and workers. They must construct storage buildings, lodging for workers, and offices. Power plants and power lines must be installed. Like any business involving hundreds of people, oil well operations create a massive amount of garbage. Aging pipelines, such as those in Siberia and Alaska, that transport oil for hundreds of miles can leak and contaminate a large area of land.

Mining

The tundra is rich in mineral deposits, many of which are still being discovered. Minerals mined in tundra around the world include coal, tin, copper, titanium, tungsten, diamonds, nickel, lead, and uranium, to name just a few. Mining requires digging deep holes in Earth's crust. When disrupted, tundra soil is usually unable to sustain plant life. It takes many years for vegetation to return to the area. Mining results in tailings, or piles of discarded minerals. Tailings can accumulate and contaminate the soil.

In the late 1800s, word spread that gold was discovered near Nome, Alaska. By 1898, there were between twenty-five thousand and thirty thousand people in Nome, making it Alaska's first urban center. The majority of these people left in the next few years, having found no gold. Their presence, however, damaged much of the ecosystem.

Recreation

More and more people these days show interest in visiting the tundra. While tourists may bring welcome money, they also bring increased pollution from cars, planes, and ships. Tourists can harm native species by disturbing nesting grounds and even taking souvenirs from the tundra. Ski resorts have become a booming business in the Alpine tundra. Unfortunately, they can also have a negative effect on the environment. On the other hand, responsible ecotourism businesses are working to preserve and protect native environments while educating tourists about threats to the tundra.

CHAPTER 5

THE FUTURE OF THE TUNDRA

The tundra is in danger. Many threats to the tundra—some of which were discussed in the previous chapter—are caused by humans. Others are the result of natural cycles. Perhaps the greatest threat to the future of the tundra is global warming.

What Is Global Warming?

Earth's atmosphere contains gases that trap heat from the sun. This process, called the greenhouse effect, keeps Earth's surface warm enough to sustain life. Without the greenhouse effect, Earth would be a frozen, lifeless planet.

Greenhouse gases include carbon dioxide, water vapor, and other gases. Earth recycles these gases naturally. Plants take in carbon dioxide as they grow, and they release it into the atmosphere where they die. However, since the Industrial Revolution, people have been burning enormous amounts of fossil fuels, such as coal and oil. These fuels are the ancient remains of plants that have died and were buried. The carbon dioxide that they contained remained trapped in Earth's crust. Burning fossil fuels releases large quantities of carbon dioxide. As a result, Earth's atmosphere contains more greenhouse gases than it can recycle.

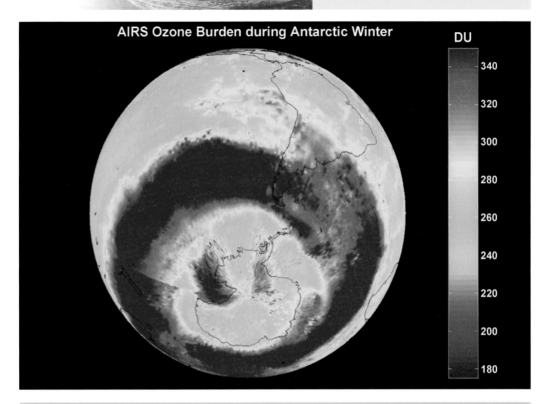

This picture was taken with an instrument called the Atmospheric Infrared Sounder, which is aboard a NASA satellite. It shows the hole in the ozone layer over Antarctica in late 2005.

Earth's climate goes through cycles. Earth has had at least four major ice ages and numerous minor ice ages. Between ice ages, the cycle swings in the opposite direction, and Earth becomes warmer. Presently, average temperatures on Earth are warmer than they have ever been in recorded history. Although this is part of Earth's cycle, temperatures are rising faster than at any other time in the last ten thousand years. Many scientists believe excess greenhouse gases are causing this drastic rise in temperature. Others, however, still maintain that it's just Earth's natural cycle and not the fault of burning fossil fuels.

How Could Global Warming Affect the Tundra?

You may have guessed that an increase in temperature is not a good thing for the tundra—a biome dependant upon continuously low temperatures. As the temperature rises, the winter season in the tundra will become shorter. Ice that has existed for thousands of years in the Arctic and Antarctic will melt. So will permafrost. This melting may cause widespread flooding in the tundra and around the world. Such drastic changes to the nonliving environment will cause native wildlife to die out. Migration patterns will change, as animals will need to move elsewhere to find enough food to survive. In northern Canada and northern Russia, the effects of global warming are already evident. Spruce trees are growing where they have never been able to survive in recorded history. This means the tree line is moving north, and the amount of tundra is decreasing.

Acid Rain

Burning fossil fuels puts other dangerous chemicals into the atmosphere, such as sulfuric acid and nitric acid. In heavily polluted areas around the world, these chemicals can fall from the sky when it rains. Acid rain—as this chemically saturated rain is commonly called—can damage the ecosystem of the Alpine tundra. It can burn lichens, mosses, and grasses. Without these basic tundra plants, many animals will die of starvation.

Endangered Species

Due to global warming, over-hunting, and destruction of the environment through industrial activities, many tundra species face extinction. Despite efforts to protect the tundra and its wildlife, endangered and threatened species include lichens, mosses, polar bears, musk oxen, caribou, whales, wolves, seabirds, seals, and sea lions.

THE PLIGHT OF THE POLAR BEAR

In the past decade, the number of polar bears has reduced drastically. As temperatures rise, Arctic ice that polar bears depend upon is beginning to melt. Polar bears travel from one floating ice floe to another in search of food. As the distances between Arctic ice floes increase, polar bears have to swim even farther to reach them. Many polar bears drown trying to do so. Others starve to death. Some scientists predict that at the rate it is melting, Arctic ice could be gone as early as 2013. Without Arctic ice, there will be no wild polar bears. In addition to this looming problem, some poachers hunt polar bears for their pelts, which sometimes sell for thousands of dollars.

Fortunately, there are many concerned people who want to save the polar bears. Polar Bears International (PBI) is a nonprofit, international group that is dedicated to the conservation and protection of polar bears around the world. Canadian wildlife photographer Dan Guravich organized PBI in 1992. Guravich passed away in 1997, but others have followed his lead in the research and careful observation of polar bear populations.

A mother polar bear rests with her cub in Bernard Spit, Alaska.

Many states, including California, have passed new laws that require auto-makers to reduce harmful emissions in the coming decade. This may help reduce the effects of global warming and protect the tundra from further harm.

Fortunately, countries that have tundra have made progress in protecting the land and its species. The list of animals that it is illegal to hunt is increasing. Many countries have established national and international reserves in the tundra to improve the chances of survival for endangered species. Native groups and nongovernmental organizations, such as the International Arctic Science Committee (IASC), are working very hard to learn more about the tundra and educate people about the dangers it faces.

What Can We Do to Protect the Tundra?

In addition to the ongoing efforts of government, nonprofit organizations, native groups, and scientific organizations, individuals can work to help save the tundra as well. There is a lot a single person can do to help reduce the biggest threat to the tundra right now, global warming. First, everyone needs to be conscious of his or her carbon footprint, which is a measure of the amount of greenhouse gases each person is responsible for releasing into the atmosphere. There are many ways to reduce your carbon footprint. You can drive less or carpool. You can keep your heat lower in the winter and air conditioners lower in the summer. You can avoid plastic products, especially bottled water, which require enormous quantities of oil to produce, transport, and clean up.

As individuals, we can also avoid buying products that are made from tundra plants and animals, except for maybe articles made by native groups for the purpose of raising money to help the tundra. When traveling to the tundra, remember to respect the biome and keep it safe from harm. Educating others about the tundra can also help. Working together, we may be able to preserve the world's most fragile biome.

alga An organism that is similar to plants but doesn't have true leaves, stems, and roots.

boreal forest Another name for the taiga biome.

buoyant Tending to float.

ecotourism A tourism trend marked by a concerned approach to ecological problems, native wildlife, and cultural traditions.

endemic Referring to something or someone that belongs in a particular region.

fungus An organism that reproduces by spores and absorbs nutrients from organic matter.

geometric Conforming to the laws of geometry.

glacier A large body of ice and compacted snow that forms in mountain valleys and at the poles.

ice age A period of time when temperatures fell worldwide and large areas of Earth's surface were covered with glaciers.

insulate To prevent or reduce the loss of heat by surrounding something with a heat-trapping material.

latitude An imaginary line joining points on Earth's surface that are all of equal distance north or south of the equator.

microorganism A tiny organism that can only be seen under a microscope.

perennial A plant that lasts for two or more growing seasons.

plateau A hill or mountain with a level top.

poacher Somebody who hunts or fishes illegally.

polygon A geometrical plane figure with three or more straight sides.

taiga A biome characterized by coniferous forests just south of the Arctic tundra.

vascular plant A plant that has an internal system for transporting fluids.

Arctic National Wildlife Refuge (ANWR)
101 12th Avenue, Room 236
Fairbanks, AK 99701
(800) 362-4546
Web site: http://arctic.fws.gov
This is a national wildlife refuge in northeastern Alaska.

All Things Arctic
P.O. Box 383
Jackson, NH 03846
(866) 556-7528
Web site: http://www.allthingsarctic.com
This is an online retailer of Arctic-related products, from clothes
    to travel packages. It's also a detailed source of information
    about the Arctic.

Environmental Defense Fund (EDF)
257 Park Avenue South
New York, NY 10010
(800) 684-3322
Web site: http://www.edf.org
The EDF is a nonprofit environmental advocacy group. Since
    1967, it's worked to improve environmental problems,
    including global warming and unsafe drinking water.

Environmental Literacy Council
1625 K Street NW, Suite 1020
Washington, DC 20006-3868
(202) 296-0390
Web site: http://www.enviroliteracy.org

This nonprofit organization is dedicated to teaching people, especially young people, the importance of protecting the environment and the biomes of the world.

International Arctic Science Committee (IASC)
P.O. Box 50003
104 05 Stockholm, Sweden
+46 8 673 96 13
Web site: http://www.arcticportal.org/iasc
The IASC is a nongovernmental, international organization whose aim is to encourage and facilitate cooperation in all aspects of Arctic research.

Polar Bears International (PBI)
105 Morris Street, Suite 188
Sebastopol, CA 95472
Web site: http://www.polarbearsinternational.org
PBI is an international, nonprofit organization dedicated to the research and protection of polar bears worldwide.

Web Sites

Due to the changing nature of Internet links, Rosen Publishing has developed an online list of Web sites related to the subject of this book. This site is updated regularly. Please use this link to access the list:

http://www.rosenlinks.com/biom/tund

Johnson, Rebecca L. *A Walk in the Tundra*. Minneapolis, MN: Carolrhoda Books, 2001.

Rosing, Norbert. *The World of the Polar Bear*. Buffalo, NY: Firefly Books, 2006.

Sale, Richard. *A Complete Guide to Arctic Wildlife*. Buffalo, NY: Firefly Books, 2006.

Squire, Ann O. *Lemmings*. New York, NY: Scholastic, 2007.

Tocci, Salvatore. *Alpine Tundra: Life on the Tallest Mountain*. London, UK: Franklin Watts, 2005.

Tocci, Salvatore. *Arctic Tundra: Life at the North Pole*. London, UK: Franklin Watts, 2005.

Warhol, Tom. *Tundra*. Salt Lake City, UT: Benchmark Books, 2007.

Williams, Suzanne M. *The Inuit*. London, UK: Franklin Watts, 2004.

Woodford, Chris. *Arctic Tundra and Polar Deserts*. Chicago, IL: Raintree, 2003.

BIBLIOGRAPHY

Arctic National Wildlife Refuge. "Ice Wedges, Polygons, and Pingos." February 14, 2006. Retrieved February 22, 2008 (http://Arctic.fws.gov/permcycl.htm).

Baldwin, Carol. *Living in the Tundra*. Chicago, IL: Heinemann Library, 2004.

De Schutter, Paul. "Palsas and Lithalsas." Open University Geological Society Mainland Europe. November 2005. Retrieved February 21, 2008 (http://ougseurope.org/rockon/surface/palsas.asp).

De Schutter, Paul. "Pingos." Open University Geological Society Mainland Europe. November 2004. Retrieved February 21, 2008 (http://ougseurope.org/rockon/surface/pingos.asp).

FightGlobalWarming.com. "The Basics of Global Warming." Environmental Defense Fund. Retrieved March 6, 2008 (http://www.fightglobalwarming.com/page.cfm?tagID=273).

Folch, Ramon. *Encyclopedia of the Biosphere: Lakes, Islands, and the Poles*. Farmington Hills, MI: The Gale Group, 2000.

Gifford, Clive, and Jerry Cadle. *The Kingfisher Young People's Book of Living Worlds*. New York, NY: Kingfisher, 2002.

Lavers, Chris. "Tundra." *Microsoft Encarta Online Encyclopedia*. 2007. Retrieved March 3, 2008 (http://au.encarta.msn.com/encyclopedia_761557297/Tundra.html).

Science Daily. "Tundra Disappearing at Rapid Rate." March 7, 2007. Retrieved March 6, 2008 (http://www.sciencedaily.com/releases/2007/03/070305140830.htm).

Somervill, Barbara A. *Tundra*. Maple Plain, MN: Tradition Books, 2004.

Walsh, Bryan. "Polar Bears Wait-Listed as Endangered." *Time*, January 12, 2008. Retrieved March 6, 2008 (http://www.time.com/time/health/article/0,8599,1704808,00.html).

Warhol, Tom. *Tundra*. Tarrytown, NY: Marshall Cavendish Benchmark, 2007.

Whitfield, Philip, Peter D. Moore, and Barry Cox. *Biomes and Habitats*. New York, NY: Macmillan Reference, 2002.

Wynn, Graeme. *Canada and Arctic North America: An Environmental History*. Santa Barbara, CA: ABC-CLIO, Inc., 2007.

INDEX

About the Author

Greg Roza has written and edited educational materials for children for the past eight years. He has a master's degree in English from the State University of New York at Fredonia. Roza has long had an interest in scientific topics, and he spends much of his spare time tinkering with machines around the house. He lives in Hamburg, New York, with his wife, Abigail, and his three children, Autumn, Lincoln, and Daisy.

Photo Credits

Designer: Les Kanturek; Editor: Nicholas Croce
Photo Researcher: Cindy Reiman